A Joel Schumacher Film

Andrew Lloyd Webber's

# The PHANTOM of the O

ISBN 0-634-09909-4

HAL•LEONARD®
CORPORATION
7777 W. BLUEMOUND RD. P.O. BOX 13819 MILWAUKEE, WI 53213

Visit Hal Leonard Online at
**www.halleonard.com**

## Andrew Lloyd Webber
### Composer, Book & Orchestrations

Andrew Lloyd Webber is the composer of *Joseph and the Amazing Technicolor Dreamcoat, Jesus Christ Superstar, By Jeeves, Evita, Variations* and *Tell Me on a Sunday* later combined as *Song & Dance, Cats, Starlight Express, The Phantom of the Opera, Aspects of Love, Sunset Boulevard, Whistle Down the Wind, The Beautiful Game* and *The Woman in White*. He composed the film scores of *Gumshoe* and *The Odessa File*, and a setting of the Latin Requiem Mass *Requiem* for which he won a Grammy for Best Contemporary Composition.

He has also produced in the West End and on Broadway not only his own work but the Olivier award-winning plays *La Bête* and *Daisy Pulls it Off*. In summer 2002 in London he presented the groundbreaking A R Rahman musical *Bombay Dreams*. He has recently completed the film version of *The Phantom of the Opera* directed by Joel Schumacher for release in December of this year.

His awards include seven Tonys, three Grammys, six Oliviers, a Golden Globe, an Oscar, an International Emmy, the Praemium Imperiale and the Richard Rodgers Award for Excellence in Musical Theatre.

He was knighted in 1992 and created an honorary life peer in 1997.

## Charles Hart
### Lyrics

Charles Hart was born in London and educated in Maidenhead and Cambridge. He has written words for musicals (*The Phantom of the Opera, Aspects of Love*), opera (*The Vampyr*, BBC 2) and miscellaneous songs, as well as both words and music for television (*Watching* and *Split Ends*, Granada TV) and radio (*Love Songs*, BBC Radio 2). Other work includes radio presenting, vocal coaching, accompanying, musical direction, musical arrangement and translation, and from 1990 – 1993 he served as a council member for the British Academy of Songwriters, Composers and Authors. He is the recipient of two Ivor Novello Awards and has been twice nominated for a Tony award.

## Richard Stilgoe
### Additional Lyrics & Book

Richard Stilgoe has spent the last year as High Sheriff of Surrey. This ancient office involves wearing black velvet and lace while trying to keep the crime rate down.

He was brought up in Liverpool, where he appeared at the Cavern Club on Saturdays and as a member of St Agnes' Church Choir on Sundays. A Choral Exhibition took him to Cambridge where all thoughts of a serious musical career were erased. The sixties found him singing his songs in pubs and nightclubs, and on Radio 4's *Today Programme*. He spent the seventies in people's living rooms via *Nationwide, That's Life* and several series of his own. In the eighties he wrote musicals. For Andrew Lloyd Webber he wrote the words for a snippet of *Cats*, almost all of *Starlight Express* and a third of *The Phantom of the Opera*. For the National Youth Music Theatre, he wrote the words and music of *Bodywork* and *Brilliant the Dinosaur*.

In 1982, he and Peter Skellern both appeared in the Royal Variety Performance. While standing star-struck in the wings watching Ethel Merman, each of them said 'We really ought to do something together sometime'. This year sees the first of several farewell tours.

Alongside all this has grown an increasing determination to make music available to more young people. To this end he founded the Orpheus Trust, which gives disabled people opportunities to make music, and this year opened the Orpheus Centre, a permanent home for this work. He is a member of the Government's Music Trust, and has presented the *Schools Proms* at the Royal Albert Hall for the last eleven years. This year the *Stilgoe Saturday Concerts* for children start at the Festival Hall, and his new musical about foxes, entitled *The Day the Earth Moved*, has its first performance.

He has won three Monte Carlo Radio prizes, the Prix Italia and an OBE. His hobbies are architecture, cricket, sailing, his five children and twin grandsons, and he looks forward to spending the next century with them.

## Joel Schumacher
### Director

Writer and Director Joel Schumacher has become one of America's most successful filmmakers. In 1995, he brought moviegoers the biggest domestic box office hit of the year, *Batman Forever*. The epic adventure-fantasy amassed a worldwide gross of more than $330 million. He next directed its successful fourth instalment, *Batman and Robin*, starring George Clooney as Batman and Arnold Schwarzenegger as Mr. Freeze.

Previous to *Batman Forever*, Schumacher directed the critically-acclaimed hit version of the John Grisham novel, *The Client*, starring Susan Sarandon and Tommy Lee Jones. In 1996, he directed the highly successful adaptation of another Grisham novel, *A Time To Kill*, starring Matthew McConaughey, Samuel L. Jackson, Sandra Bullock and Kevin Spacey.

Schumacher's features, such as *St. Elmo's Fire, The Lost Boys, Cousins* and *Flatliners* starring Julia Roberts, have displayed the filmmaker's versatility and close attention to performance, nuance and atmosphere. *Dying Young* reunited Schumacher and Julia Roberts. He followed this up with the gritty, controversial *Falling Down*, starring Michael Douglas.

In 1999 Schumacher directed the thriller *8MM*, starring Nicolas Cage. Also in 1999 he wrote and directed *Flawless*, starring Robert De Niro and Philip Seymour Hoffman. In 2000 he directed *Tigerland*, about young men training for Vietnam in 1971, as well as *Phone Booth*, both starring Colin Farrell. He then went on to direct *Bad Company* starring Anthony Hopkins and Chris Rock for Jerry Bruckheimer Films and Disney, which was released in June of 2002. Most recently Joel directed Cate Blanchett in *Veronica Guerin*, the true story of the Irish journalist killed by Dublin's drug lords, also for Disney and Bruckheimer.

Joel Schumacher was born and raised in New York City, where he studied design and display at Parsons School of Design. He began his career in the entertainment industry as an art director for television commercials before becoming costume designer for such notable films as Woody Allen's *Sleeper* and *Interiors*, Herbert Ross's *The Last of Sheila* and Paul Mazursky's *Blume In Love*. He then wrote the screenplays for *Sparkle* and the hit comedy *Car Wash*.

Schumacher made his directing debut with the television movie *The Virginia Hill Story*, starring Dyan Cannon in the title role and Harvey Keitel as the mobster Bugsy Siegel. This was followed by his award-winning tele-film *Amateur Night at the Dixie Bar and Grill*. *The Incredible Shrinking Woman*, starring Lily Tomlin, marked his feature film directing debut, followed by *D.C. Cab*, for which he also wrote the screenplay. Schumacher also wrote the script for *St. Elmo's Fire* with Carl Kurlander. In 1988, Schumacher directed the successful Chicago theatrical run of David Mamet's scorching Hollywood satire, "*Speed-the-Plow*."

Published by
**The Really Useful Group Limited**
22 Tower Street, London WC2H 9TW
www.reallyuseful.com

EXCLUSIVELY DISTRIBUTED BY

7777 W. BLUEMOUND RD. P.O. BOX 13819 MILWAUKEE, WI 53213

ISBN: 0-634-09909-4

This edition is comprised of works written for the original stage production of
THE PHANTOM OF THE OPERA
together with three new works, 'The Fairground', 'Journey To The Cemetery'
and 'Learn To Be Lonely', which were specifically written for the movie.

All music arranged by Roger Day except 'The Fairground', 'Journey To The Cemetery'
and 'Learn To Be Lonely', arranged by David Cullen
Music processed by Paul Ewers Music Design

Photographs by Alex Bailey

Book designed by Dewynters, London

# THINK OF ME

**Music by ANDREW LLOYD WEBBER**
**Lyrics by CHARLES HART**
**Additional lyrics by RICHARD STILGOE**

Think of me, think of me fond-ly when we've said good-bye. Re-mem-ber me once in a while,_ please pro-mise me you'll try.

When you find ___ that once a - gain you long ___ to take your heart back and be free, if you ev - er find a mo - ment, spare a thought for me.

We nev-er said___ our love was ev-er-green___ or as un-chang-ing as the sea, but if you can still re-mem-ber, stop and think of me. Think of all the things we've shared and seen; don't think a-bout the way things

day when I won't think of you.

RAOUL
Can it be,
can it be Christ - ine
Long a - go___ it seems so
long a - go,___ how young and in - no - cent we were. She may not re-mem - ber

# ANGEL OF MUSIC

**Music by ANDREW LLOYD WEBBER**
**Lyrics by CHARLES HART**
**Additional lyrics by RICHARD STILGOE**

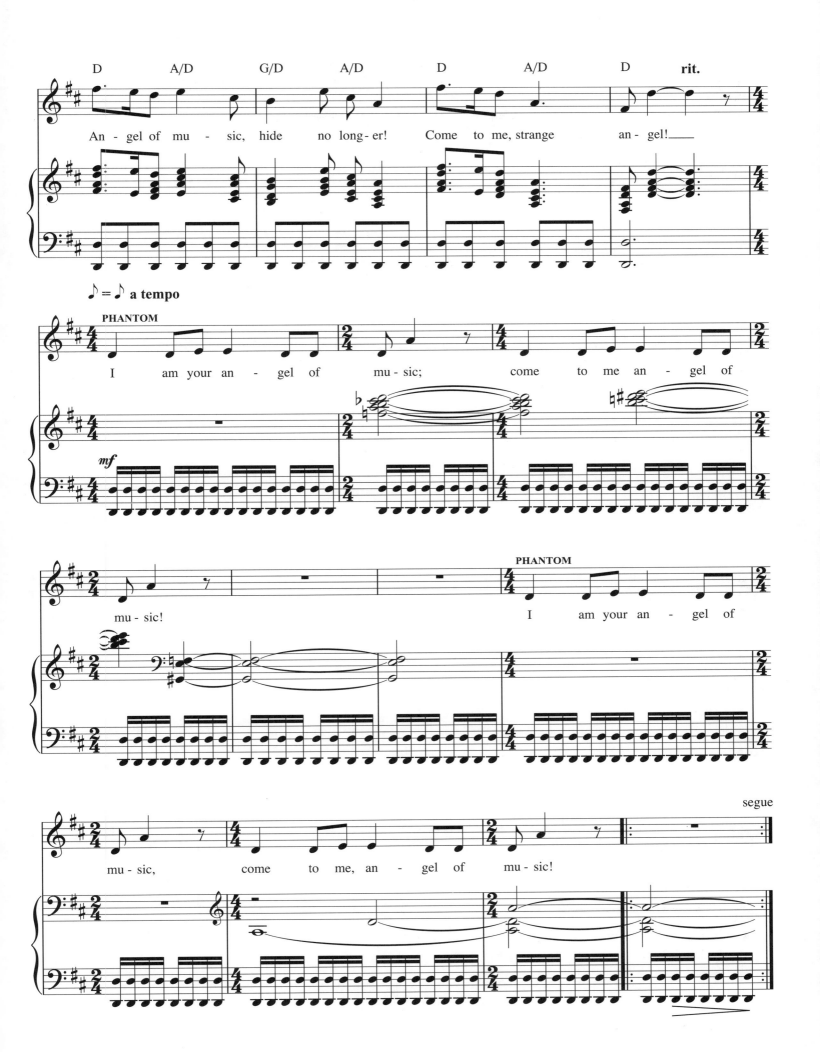

An - gel of mu - sic, hide no long - er! Come to me, strange an - gel!____

PHANTOM
I am your an - gel of mu - sic; come to me an - gel of mu - sic!

PHANTOM
I am your an - gel of mu - sic, come to me, an - gel of mu - sic!

# THE PHANTOM OF THE OPERA

**Music by ANDREW LLOYD WEBBER**
*Lyrics by CHARLES HART*
Additional lyrics by RICHARD STILGOE & MIKE BATT

26

phan - tom of the op - era._____ Be - ware the

phan - tom of the op - era._____

11/16/09

In all your fan - ta - sies,_____ you al - ways

**PHANTOM**

knew_____ that man and mys - ter - y_____ were both in you.

**CHRISTINE**

29

He's there the phan-tom of the op-era. Ah!

Sing, my angel, sing!

Ah!

(1°) Sing for me!

32

# THE MUSIC OF THE NIGHT

**Music by ANDREW LLOYD WEBBER**
**Lyrics by CHARLES HART**
**Additional lyrics by RICHARD STILGOE**

34

35

**a tempo**

night. Let your mind start a jour-ney through a strange, new world; leave all

thoughts of the life you knew be - fore. Let your soul take you where you long to

be! On - ly then can you be - long to me.

**a tempo**

Float - ing, fall - ing, sweet in-tox-i-ca - tion. Touch me, trust me, sa-vour each sen-sa - tion.

# PRIMA DONNA

**Music by ANDREW LLOYD WEBBER**
**Lyrics by CHARLES HART**
**Additional lyrics by RICHARD STILGOE**

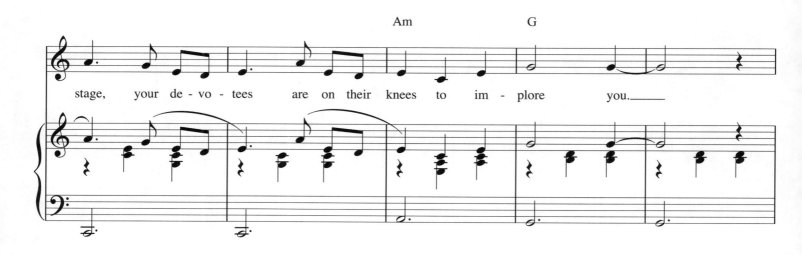

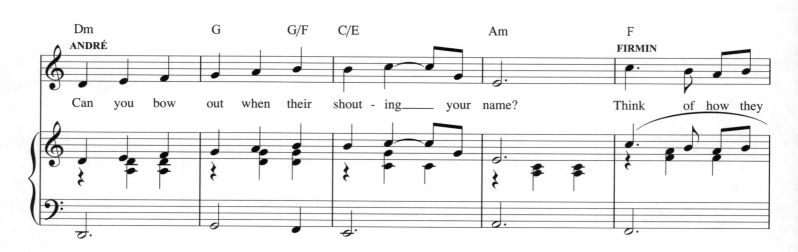

41

-gain and to un-end-ing o-va - tion.

Think how you'll shine in that fi - nal en-core; sing;

Pri - ma Don-na, once more!

**ANDRÉ & FIRMIN**

Who'd be-lieve a di-va hap-py to re-lieve a cho-rus girl who's gone and slept with the pa - tron?

Raoul and the soub-rette en-twined in love's du - et; al-though he may de-mur he must have been with her. You'd

nev - er get a - way with all this in a play, but if it's loud-ly sung and in a for-eign tongue, it's

just the sort of sto - ry au - dien-ces a - dore, in fact a per - fect op - era.

Pri - ma Don - na, the world is at your feet, a na - tion

# ALL I ASK OF YOU

Music by ANDREW LLOYD WEBBER
Lyrics by CHARLES HART
Additional lyrics by RICHARD STILGOE

here, with you, be-side you, to guard you and to guide you.

CHRISTINE
Say you love me ev-'ry wak-ing mo-ment, turn my head with talk of sum-mer-time.

Say you need me with you now and al-ways; pro-mise me that all you say is true, that's all I ask of

49

50

# MASQUERADE

**Music by ANDREW LLOYD WEBBER**
**Lyrics by CHARLES HART**
**Additional lyrics by RICHARD STILGOE**

# THE FAIRGROUND

**Composed by ANDREW LLOYD WEBBER**

# JOURNEY TO THE CEMETERY

**Composed by ANDREW LLOYD WEBBER**

**Moderato**

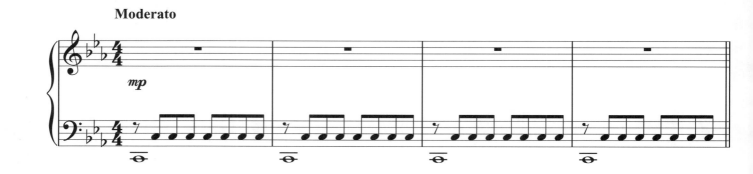

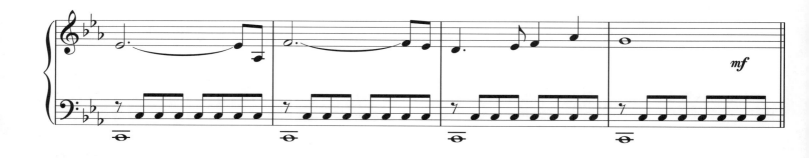

# WISHING YOU WERE SOMEHOW HERE AGAIN

**Music by ANDREW LLOYD WEBBER**
**Lyrics by CHARLES HART**
**Additional lyrics by RICHARD STILGOE**

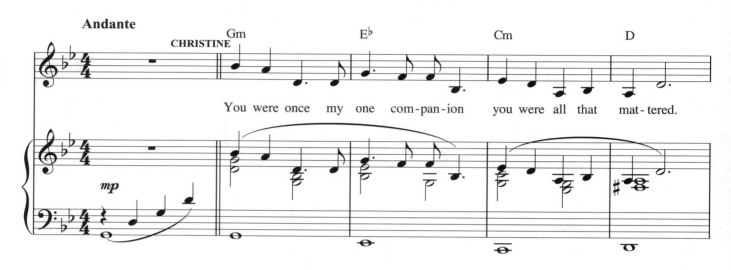

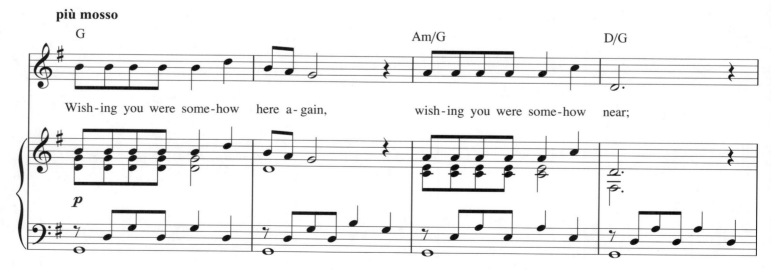

seem for you the wrong com-pan-ions; you were warm and gen-tle.

Too ma-ny years fight-ing back tears, why can't the past just die?

Wish-ing you were some-how here a-gain, know-ing we must say good-

bye.    Try to for-give,    teach me to live,    give me the strength to

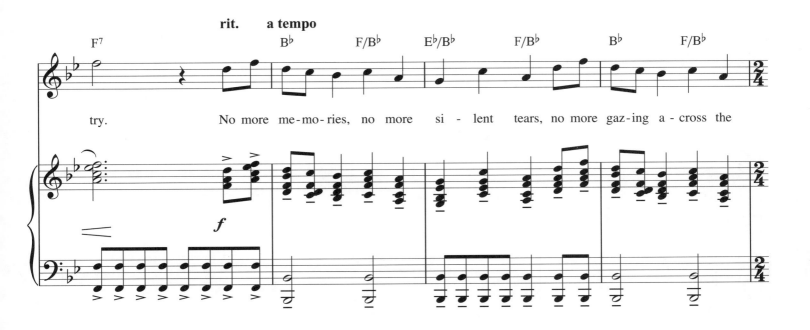

try.    No more me-mo-ries, no more si - lent tears, no more gaz-ing a-cross the

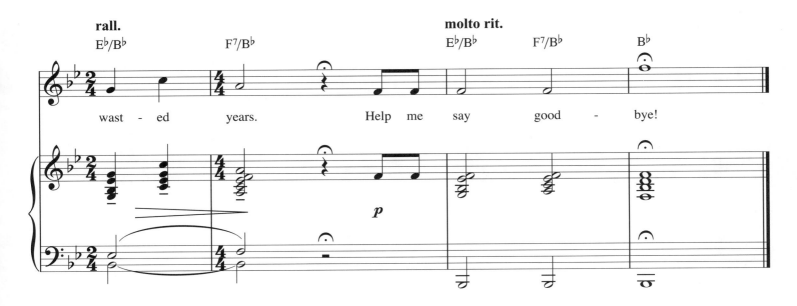

wast - ed years.    Help me say good - bye!

# THE POINT OF NO RETURN

**Music by ANDREW LLOYD WEBBER**
**Lyrics by CHARLES HART**
**Additional lyrics by RICHARD STILGOE**

**Andante (♩.)**

PHANTOM (AS DON JUAN)

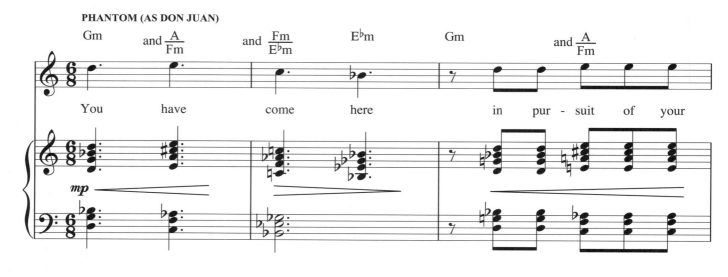

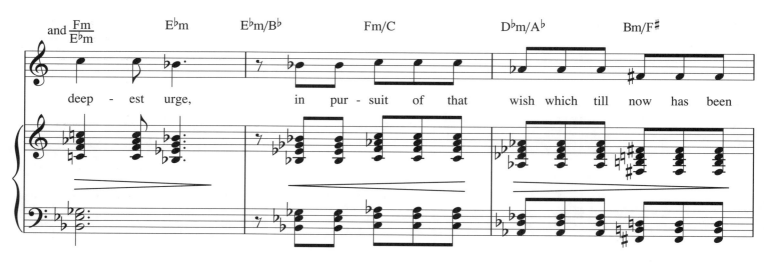

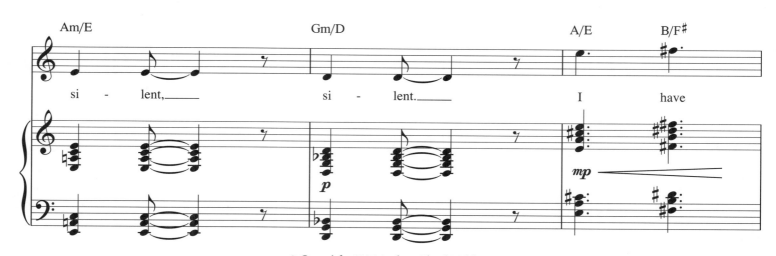

CHRISTINE (AS AMINTA)

**a tempo 1°**

no re - turn? You have brought me to that mo-ment where words run dry, to that mo-ment where speech dis-ap-pears in-to si - lence,___ si - lence.___ I have come here hard-ly know-ing the rea - son why, in my mind I've al - rea - dy i - ma-gined our

# LEARN TO BE LONELY

**Music by ANDREW LLOYD WEBBER**
**Lyrics by CHARLES HART**